I Saw Some Angels Today…

Monique DeCicco-Jones

Illustrations By:

Angelina DeCicco-Jones

This book is dedicated to the angels that graced my presence on the morning of July 4, 2020.

I saw some angels today,

I was surprised in every

which way.

I saw some angels today,

They didn't look human

in any sort of way.

A glimmer of light

With lines going through,

I rubbed my eyes to ensure

my view!

They were every which way,

not just one or two.

No visible eyes,

Just a cloud-like dew.

Each had a form,

a few lines going

through,

No harm would

come to me,

This I knew!

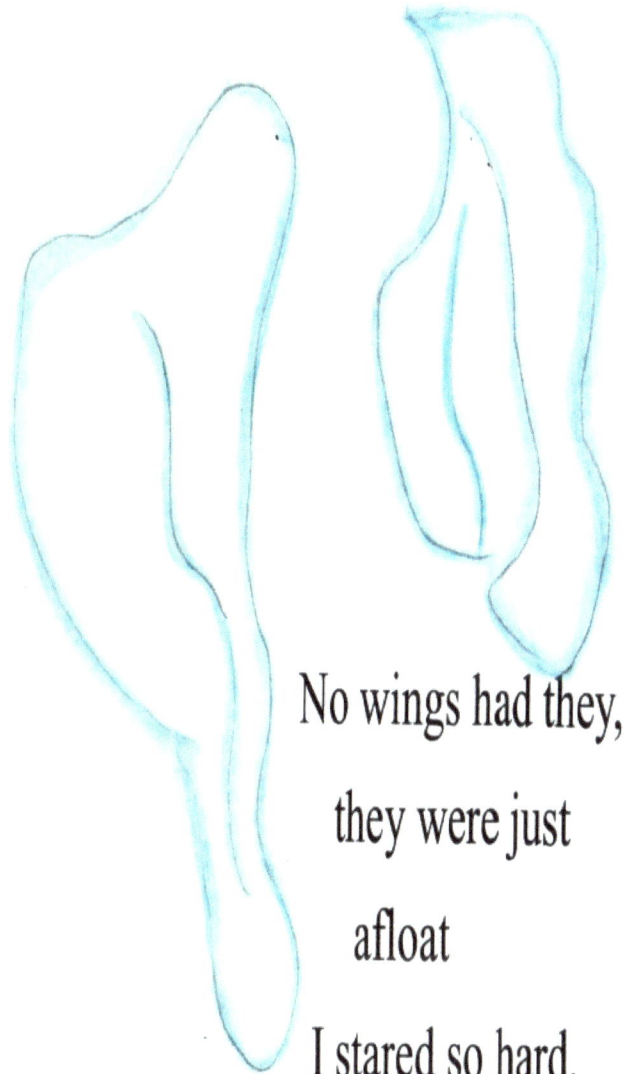

No wings had they,

they were just

afloat

I stared so hard,

I seemed to gloat!

I moved my head,

from left to right.

Bedazzled by…

the incredible sight!

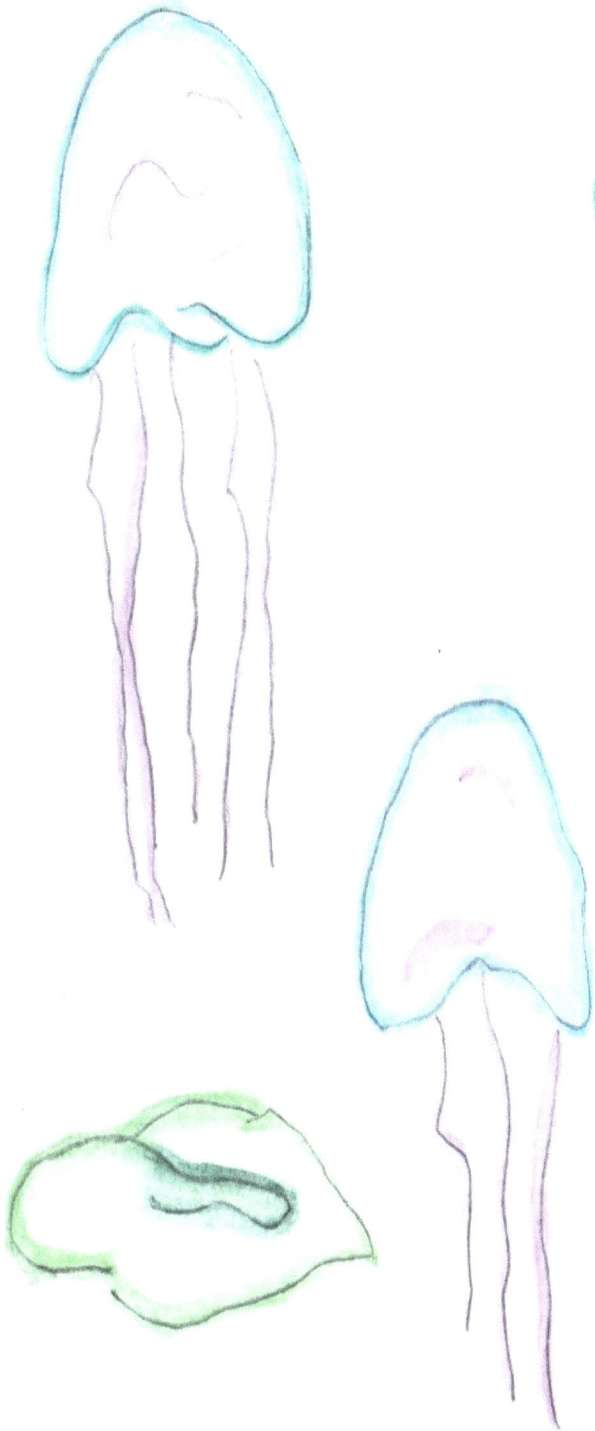

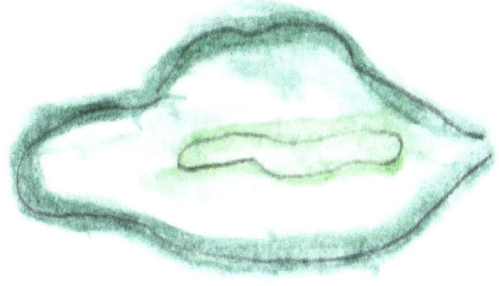

There is nothing earthly,

to compare them to.

Except tadpoles or jellyfish,

or something see-through.

I spent all day wondering,

what it is that they do.

Why had I seen them?

I wish that I knew!

I asked myself ...

"What did I eat?"

"What did I drink?"

That would allow

me to see them,

I had to think!

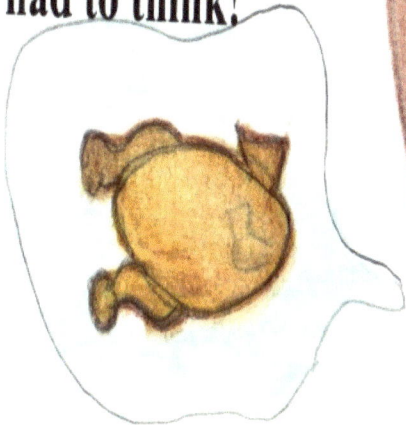

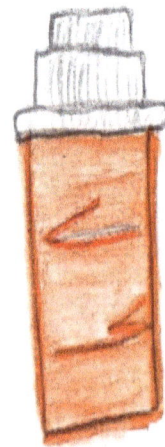

Nothing out the ordinary,

just a few vitamins.

Nothing that could've led

to an x-ray-like lens.

I saw some angels today…

It left me perplexed.

I wondered and wondered …

What could possibly be next?

It took 48 years,

And a dark early morning

To open my eyes,

and see this sight dawning!

They were everywhere,
floating over my bed…
Not one word spoken,
not one word said.

After much thought,

I became so confused.

Were they angels or aliens?

How would I choose?

I had never seen either,

What did I know?

Only stories from the Bible,

That I keep in tow.

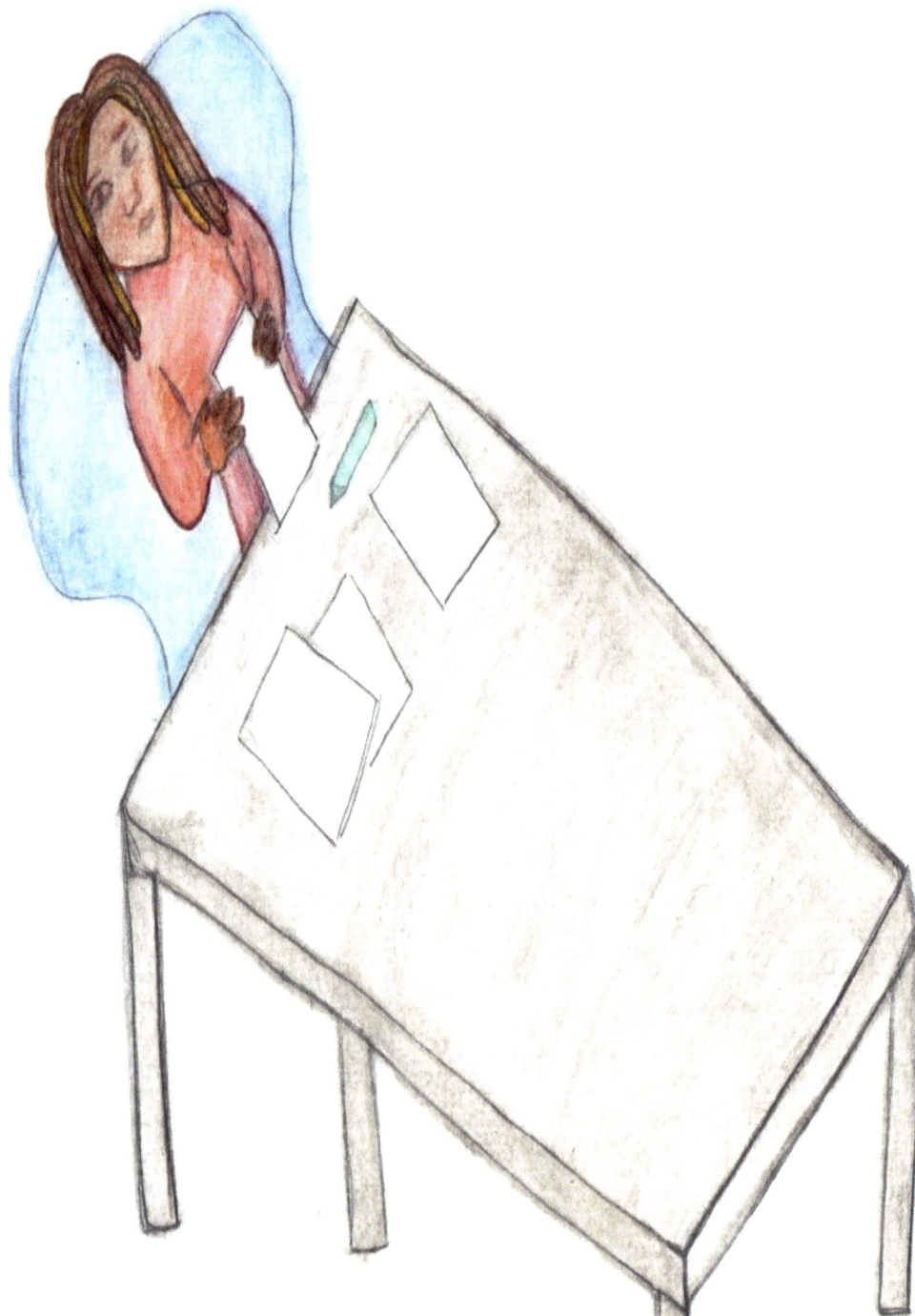

I had never seen either,

Nor did anyone I know.

So I ran to the Bible,

Some research to go!

Angels were in there!

No mention of aliens at all....

I read through Matthew, Mark, Luke, John

and the epistles of Paul!

Old testament and new,

I checked the "Good Book"

through and through!

Revelation 12:13
1 Thessalonians 4:16
Genesis 1:26
Genesis 16: 7-14
Genesis 22: 11-15
Exodus 3: 2-4
Numbers 22: 22-38
Judges 2: 1-3
Judges 6: 11-23
Judges 13: 3-22
Zechariah 1:12
Jude 6
Ezekiel 1 and 10
Daniel 10: 13-21
Daniel 12:1
Jude 9
Hebrew 1:14
Daniel 10:21
Daniel 6: 20-23
Revelation 12:17
Revelation 9

Matthew 28:4
Titus 1:2
Genesis 21: 17-20
Genesis 6:4
Genesis 19:1
Genesis 18
Genesis 19
Daniel 9:21
Isaiah 6:1-13

Luke 2
Exodus 25:20
Daniel 10:21
Judges 6: 20-24
Hebrews 1:6
Hebrews 13:2
Daniel 10: 5-6
Genesis 21

Acts 10:3
Job 38:4-7
Job 1:6
Job 2:1

Colossians 1:16
Isaiah 6:1-13
Luke 1: 26-38
Luke 2: 8-15

Holy Bible

Exodus 25:20
Matthew 24:36
Matthew 18:10
Revelations 14:6

Matthew 1:20-21
Matthew 2:13
Luke 1: 11-20
Luke 2:13-14

1 Peter 1:12
James 2:11
2 King 11-35
Luke 8: 28-31
2 Samuel 24:15-16
2 Timothy 2:26
Matthew 1-2
Ephesians 3:10
Luke 16:22
1 Corinthians 11:10
Psalms 148:1-2
1 Kings 19: 5-7
Acts 7: 52-53
Acts 12:7-11
Acts 27: 23-24
Acts 8:26
1 Corinthians 4:9
1 Corinthians 11:10
2 Kings 6:13-17
Psalms 103:20

Revelation 7:1; 8:2
Acts 12:5-10
Acts 8:26
Revelation 5:8-13

Then I went to science…

For an answer to my sight.

Only hypotheses were there,

that hadn't been proven right!

=

+

Heavenly bodies described...

Both these I knew,

Perhaps they were the same

One in the two !

So I asked myself:
What could aliens
want with me?"
They had to be
angels!
Would else could
they be?

To all non-believers,

Angels ARE real!

Actually seeing them,

I now knew the deal!

I saw some angels today…

A sight never to be forgotten.

They were opaque,

With a dim light.

That gradually faded …

From my sight!

I saw some angels today…

This is a true account of an apparition appearing to the author on the early morning of July 4, 2020.

While designed for children, this book encourages the reading of listed Bible verses on angels' appearances in the Bible and can be enjoyed by children and adults alike.

Monique DeCicco-Jones is a freelance writer, editor, and publisher as well as a realtor in Georgia, ordained minister, and nurse practitioner in New York State. She enjoys life with her family and lives in both Savannah, Georgia and Liberty, NY.

Angelina DeCicco-Jones is a 13-year-old illustrator in the 8th grade at St. James Catholic School is Savannah, Georgia. She enjoys art, volleyball, and vacationing!

$9.99
ISBN 978-1-7357134-0-3
50999>

9 781735 713403

www.ingramcontent.com/pod-product-compliance
Lightning Source LLC
Chambersburg PA
CBHW040025050426

42452CB00003B/141